Challenges

Why I Wrote This For You

As recruiters, we have challenges that add to the time it takes to fill a position. Plus they add to our frustration because they can keep us from doing the great recruiting we want to do. At the same time, these challenges are often invisible to everyone involved—except for us, of course!

I want to share tips, strategies and most importantly, the essential questions for you to ask. These are the things that will:

> ➤ Get your hiring manager to partner with you
> ➤ Get the search moving
> ➤ Help you end the search with a great hire and a happy hiring manager!

Just a Little About Me

Recruiting was my third career, having previously been a marketing executive for a software development firm and then running my coaching and personal development firm for several years.

I have been a corporate recruiter at Deloitte & Touche, a recruiter for Heidrick & Struggles a world-wide retained executive search company and a small regional retained recruiting firm in Orange County, CA.

In these roles, I've filled positions ranging from individual contributors to CEOs with million dollar salaries, in industries ranging from complex technologies to cupcake bakeries.

While I still do selected executive level recruiting, I love that I get to train and coach recruiters in companies across the US. Even though it means leaving my little lakeside cabin, it is so exciting to meet recruiters around the country and watch as my techniques help them fill positions faster. Even better, they report they are having more fun and enjoying more influential relationships with their hiring managers.

How to Start Benefitting Immediately

Your inner consultative recruiter will show up the moment you start using this information.

And you don't even have to read the whole book.

Pick a situation you are experiencing and start using the tips right away.

Your hiring managers won't know what you're doing but they will see and feel the new you. And you get to play an even larger role as their trusted advisor in their recruiting.

For more recruiting tips, templates and insights only we as recruiters will understand, check out The Consultative Recruiter available on Amazon.

Contact Me: Katherine@ConsultativeRecruiting.com and 832.464.4447

SITUATION	SOLUTIONS
You want to get your HMs feeling like the two of you are on the same page. **NOTE:** This isn't quite the same as getting your hiring managers to partner with you for their recruiting. If you have that challenge, see situation later in this report: Hiring managers (HMs) don't seem to take recruiting as seriously as you feel they should.	➢ *As you talk to them, every so often ask this question:* ❑ Does that make sense? ➢ This question gets people in the rhythm of saying "yes" to you, and makes it feel like the two of you are a team. ➢ Sometimes people won't say they don't believe you or that they don't agree with what you're saying. Asking this question provides a way for them to tell you what they are thinking. ➢ Plus, if the HM isn't tracking with what you're saying or maybe not even really listening, this is the best way to find out sooner than later. ➢ Building consensus helps get the hiring manager engaged with you, help build a business partnership and can smooth out bumps along the way.
HM asks a question about the candidate while reviewing a resume to which you do not have the answer.	➢ *Ask this question:* ❑ Do you need the answer before deciding if you want to move ahead with the candidate? ➢ Then stop talking and wait for the HM to answer. ➢ After they answer your question, assure the HM: "I can get that information for you." Just be careful not to imply they should wait until you get back to them before they make a decision or move the candidate forward. ➢ Variations of this question can be used in any situation where you want to keep things moving forward even though the HM (or someone else) has asked a question to which you do not have the answer handy.

HM makes a statement that is vague, seems out of left field or one that you suspect might indicate they are simply thinking out loud. So do you take it seriously, explore it with them, or walk away totally confused. If you do the latter, it is unlikely that your confusion will clear up without another conversation.	➤ *Ask this question:* ❑ Would you tell me more about that? ➤ Whenever possible, preface that question with an observation that helps build your partnership. Statements like **"That's in interesting point"** or **"I would like to hear your thoughts on that"** let the HM know you appreciate their perspective but aren't just saying OK and going away. ➤ It's important to let your HM think outloud if that is how they process information. You need to listen closely so you can distinguish between when they are thinking things through with you and when they are giving you critical information about the search. ➤ Letting your hiring manager do this kind of brainstorming can be a wonderful way to strengthen your relationship. If people are willing to share this kind of thinking with you, they are probably feeling comfortable with you and willing to listen to your thoughts, perspective and advice. ➤ If you hear something that seems to be new information or a new direction for the search, be sure to confirm that with them. **Are you rethinking the requirements?** or **So you are changing what this person will do?**,etc. ➤ This helps the hiring manager see where their statement is lacking details or substance. This is a place the hiring manager really needs you to help them think it through. ➤ Those direct questions will probably get you more good information than saying the typical "**So what I hear you saying is…**" Try a couple of different questions and see what works best with your hiring manager.
HM says: Can you find more candidates? I just think I should see more.	➤ There can be many reasons the hiring manager wants to see a lot of candidates.

This often means your hiring manager has:
1. Unexpressed things they are hoping to find in a candidate; and/or
2. Fear of making a hiring mistake, so they keep interviewing until they get that "gut feel" that makes them feel confident.
3. Concerns that you haven't managed to land the best candidates or have somehow missed finding them.

➢ They may assume tons of people would be interested and feel a slight sense you didn't **do the job** if they only see a few. Alternatively, they may be unsure of their ability to make a good hiring decision, and are waiting for that elusive "good gut feeling."

➢ The comprehensive Launch Document facilitates a conversation to bring those reasons to light both during the launch meeting and when you are talking to them about the candidates they have seen. (I've included my Launch Document for you at the end of this book.)

➢ It's important for you to get as much information as possible about what has caused the HM to come to this conclusion.

➢ Ask these questions:
  ❑ Are you thinking you need to just see more people or you want to see candidates with a different skill set?
  ❑ Do you have a particular number of candidates you feel you need to see before you can make a decision?
  ❑ Can you take me through what you want to see in the additional candidates that you aren't seeing so far?
  ❑ Is there anyone in the current group you've seen who should be moved forward to more interviews?

➢ Also, just because they have the title "hiring manager" doesn't mean they are good at assessing and evaluating candidates.

➢ When you ask these questions, you are also helping the HM think through their decision-making process around hiring. You may find that the hiring manager even needs your perspective around what makes a viable candidate.

➢ They may need some assistance crafting and/or evaluating interview answers. When you have a conversation and ask questions to help them think things through, you are giving them that assistance.

➢ Evaluating and assessing candidates isn't necessarily something HMs do well. These questions will help them... and keep your search moving to closure.

| Feedback from the HM after an interview is vague, non-specific, e.g., Not a fit, Didn't blow my socks off, etc. | <ul><li>There are subtle easy ways to help the hiring manager give you feedback that is actually, well, real and useful feedback! Help them go beyond the words "not a fit."</li><li>In almost every case, you'll find the hiring manager didn't give much feedback because they didn't know how to articulate beyond general vague comments like **"not a fit. I'll know it when I see it."**</li><li>That means they are hoping to have a good feeling as a way to know when they are looking at a good candidate. You have to take them through all the responsibilities and requirements set out in the launch meeting and ask very specific questions.</li><li>Ask the questions that can help the hiring manager make an assessment of the candidate. Those questions have to be very narrow, such as the ones above. Questions like **What was the problem with the candidate** are frankly too large for most hiring managers to answer with details that matter.</li><li>*Ask questions like these:*<ul><li>Can you give me an idea of what is missing with the candidate(s) you've seen?</li><li>What would it take to have you see them as a fit, blow your socks off, etc.?</li><li>Was there a particular question or did the candidate do something during the interview that made you come to that conclusion?</li><li>How did you feel the candidate stacked up against the requirements? (You may have to list each requirement to get a sense of how the HM evaluated the candidate. If you just ask the overall requirements fit, it may be too difficult for the HM to answer with enough detail to be useful to you.</li><li>How do you know when you're sitting across from a great candidate?</li><li>What is the one thing you really hope to hear a candidate say?</li></ul></li></ul> |

| HM is taking a long time to take the next step that keeps the search moving. | <ul><li>➤ *Ask this question:*<ul><li>❑ What would you recommend we tell the candidate about the reason for the delay?</li><li>❑ Is there anyone else who can meet with the candidate sooner just so we keep the candidate moving forward?</li></ul></li><li>➤ This question gets the HM to partner with you to craft a message for the candidate, and gently points out that candidates often do not just hang around forever. Now the two of you share the responsibility to keep the candidate willing to wait. If you don't do this, you will be seen as the **only** person responsible to keep the candidate circling the airport and will be the one who is seen as having lost the candidate if they do not wait.</li><li>➤ If you having a hiring manager who does things that slow the search down, you might want to ask this question in your next launch meeting:</li><li>➤ **When would you like to have this position filled?**</li><li>➤ Now of course you and I know they are probably going to answer something cute like **later today** or even **yesterday**. So you aren't asking the question because you couldn't figure out they would answer like that.</li><li>➤ You're asking so that later in the search when they start to slow down and seem to lose momentum, you can say:</li><li>➤ **When we talked initially you mentioned wanting to fill the position quickly. Has that changed for you?**</li><li>➤ Now the hard part: stop talking!</li><li>➤ It is recommended that you consider avoiding the "**we might lose the candidate**" lecture. Every HM knows that and when you say it again, they start to tune you out.</li></ul> |

9

HM does not get back to you with feedback about resumes, interviews, etc.	➤ This is one of those situations that add to your work because you have to: ❑ Keep the candidates in the loop ❑ Keep following up with the hiring manager ❑ Face the fact - delays are extending the time to fill metric.
Changing how you respond to this will: 1. Save you tons of time and 2. Create a stronger partnership with your hiring manager.	➤ Use the **"Give me a commitment technique"** I've included for you at the end of this toolkit ❑ It may take a little time for the HM to adjust to your new approach. But it will happen and save you the hassle and wasted time you used to spend just tracking them down to get feedback.
	➤ Result: ❑ In addition to keeping the search moving quickly, using this technique positions you as a business partner and trusted advisor. ❑ It's probably one of the most impactful change you can make in your relationship with the HMs.
HM has an internal candidate they want to interview, even though you are far down the road with other candidates.	➤ Obviously you've got a **"good news-bad news"** situation. ❑ **Good news** because it means an internal candidate is getting an opportunity for a new position; ❑ **Bad news** because it can delay the search, lose you candidates and add to your work load trying to keep all the pieces moving forward. ➤ *Ask this question at the **search launch** meeting:* ❑ Do you know of anyone you would like to have in the position or if anyone has indicated interest? ➤ Asking those questions may get the internal candidate into the process sooner. But even if the HM doesn't know of anyone, you have started them thinking about the internal candidate pool. ➤ When the internal candidate enters the process, talk to the HM to set some timelines for next steps. This gives you as much control as possible while getting the HM involved and committed to moving quickly on the internal candidate.

Your hiring manager delays making an offer, saying "If the candidate wants to work for us, they will wait for us even if they have another offer."	➤ *Ask this question:* ❑ What would you think is an appropriate explanation to the candidate for the delay? OR What would you like the message to the candidate to be? ➤ This question helps get the hiring manager realize they and you share responsibility for keeping candidates warm until they make a decision. ➤ If you don't do this, they will feel it is entirely up to you to keep candidates circling the airport until the hiring manager is ready to make a decision. That means they also will feel that if a great candidate withdraws or is lost to another company, you are responsible. ➤ HMs may really enjoy working for the company and think it should be self-evident to any candidate that it's the best choice for new job. ➤ Or the HM may not want to deal with how to manage the dynamics of putting a candidate on hold. **They really need you here!** ➤ Rather than react to what you hear, you will make a bigger impact if you have a **conversation** that puts the HM in the candidate's shoes.
Hiring managers (HMs) don't seem to take recruiting as seriously as you feel they should. **NOTE:** Working long hours, making lots of great placements and being totally accommodating to your hiring managers won't change this.	➤ *HMs may feel that:* ❑ Recruiting is YOUR job because running their department, function, etc., is THEIR real job ❑ It's just a matter of finding candidates - how hard can it be? ➤ This means that recruiting is viewed as order taking, not a consultative function. Interestingly, recruiting is often the one corporate function everyone else thinks they know how to do. ➤ Whatever your HMs may be thinking, you can transition them to new thinking and therefore a new higher level of participation by the actions you take with them and the information you share with them.

You need to take specific action, the best of which is to ask more questions wherein you demonstrate your value-add.	➤ *In your interactions with them:* ❑ Behave the way you feel a trusted advisor would, avoid lectures about our "process", and ask questions to engage them in expanded conversations. ❑ Be calm. Remember that pushing back doesn't get you the results you think it will. When pushed, most people will push back at you—it's human nature. As always, avoid lectures. If you've said it before, say it differently or skip it this time. ❑ Don't worry about getting the change you want the first time you suggest it. You can afford to be flexible, because with the techniques in this guide, you're always going to get better results. **LANGUAGE TIP:** Questions are your secret to building business relationships, conveying your expertise, and demonstrating your trusted advisor skills. Avoid any questions that start with **Why** because those questions can put people on the defensive. Plus **why** questions don't seem to generate answers as useful as questions that start differently. Try it!
Hiring managers don't seem to be happy with the recruiting function in general, or something you've done. **NOTE:** This approach works with anyone who may seem to be a bit at odds with you. Building stronger relationships with others who influence and/or interact with your hiring managers can help ensure you can do the great recruiting you want to do.	➤ If you have a feeling your HM is unhappy about something you've done, it's probably best to address it. ➤ It's easier to just let it go and hope they forget, or that you can get off the hot seat by working even harder. But it's in your best interest to see if you can get a few minutes of your HM's time. ➤ Tell them you would like their advice and/or perspective on something you've been observing. Or something like that which doesn't makes it sound like "We have to have **the** talk". ➤ One of the principals of building a business relationship is to address the elephant in the room. It can be done with mutual respect, and you may find the HM is relieved to get the issue on the table and resolved.

	LANGUAGE TIP: When you ask for someone's advice and/or perspective, two things happen. • First, everyone is usually honored that you want that from them. • Second, it helps you get some distance from the situation. Now it isn't a "why did you do this" kind of conversation but more about "I'm wondering how you see this situation" or "Would you give me your perspective of …"

Hiring managers don't follow the "process".	➢ It's just not possible to "mandate" that people follow a process. You can, however, guide your hiring managers in a way that will make it easier for them to follow the process one step at a time.
	
	➢ Also, since hiring managers may secretly feel recruiting is YOUR job, they may not be excited to have to follow YOUR process.
	
	➢ You may need to do what they are used to you doing at first—the old process or the process the previous recruiter let them follow. Change is a challenge for most of us. It's interesting that while HMs may not be happy with the recruiting function, they may not be excited about changing anything that could improve their results.
	
	➢ *So your conversations with them should reassure them that:*
	   ❑ You're the one making the change and
	   ❑ The new methodology will benefit them in their hiring.
	
	LANGUAGE TIP:
	Avoid the 'P' word—Process.
	• No one is eager to change, and most of us have little motivation to change in order to follow the process of someone else.
	• Skip that word in order to get more cooperation.

Hiring managers are frustrated with time the search takes	➤ Many things impact the time it takes to fill a position, and recruiters do not have control over all of them. But even things that you have no control over will be included in the recruiting measurement called "Time to fill" by which you may be evaluated and are forming the hiring manager's perception of **too long!**
	➤ For one or two searches, to point out the realities of the "time to fill" metric, keep track of the time lags when you are waiting for hiring manager feedback or hiring decision. Without throwing the hiring manager under the bus, you can now have the metrics "birds and bees" conversation.
	➤ At the beginning or launch of a search, you will want to ask some questions to uncover HM expectations about time to fill. Ask questions to explore the challenges to a fast hire. ➤ Share with the HM what you know (or anticipate based on your recruiting experience): ❑ What candidate population might look like, and ❑ How that may influence the time it takes to fill the position with a great candidate. ➤ If the candidate pool will be small, explore any requirements on which the hiring manager may be willing to be flexible. At the beginning of a search, the hiring manager may not be willing to flex on their requirements. ➤ See if they will agree to talking to you about doing that a couple of weeks after you start sourcing. That way, you'll have concrete information about the realities of the candidate pool—how many people are likely to meet the requirements and how many of them will be interested in the position as currently structured. **LANGUAGE TIP** Do this as a conversation not a lecture. Ask questions to understand how your hiring manager is thinking—even if you secretly sometimes think they are crazy! You cannot really move them to think about things your way until you understand them.

	NEVER emphatically stating that there won't be any candidates who meet the requirements. You may be right about that but if you do find some good candidates, you've painted yourself into a corner. Now presenting those candidates points out your prediction was totally wrong, and you lose some of the hiring manager's trust in your advice. Instead, suggest that you go to the candidate marketplace to see if candidates who meet the hiring manager's requirements are interested. Tell the hiring manager you will get back to them within a week to share the market's response to the position.

HMs aren't willing to try the new things you are suggesting.	➢ When you are starting to transition your recruiting to your new more consultative methodology, don't ask or expect your hiring managers to change everything immediately. You can be flexible because you know as the search progresses, they will see the tremendous advantages of the new things you're doing.
	
	➢ For example, if your hiring managers are used to having you post a job description the minute they send it to you, you may need to do that.
	
	➢ At the same time:
	  ❏ Be sure to set up a launch meeting.
	  ❏ After that meeting, show them the job posting you're written,
	  ❏ Talk a little about the advantages of that rewrite.
	  ❏ As the search goes on, demonstrate the quality and number of candidates that were attracted to the old job description versus the new job posting.

You don't get all the information you need when a new requisition is opened so searches often stop and start. For a whole bunch of reasons, they ultimately take too long.	➢ Since this is the foundation for a fast and fabulously successful search that will end with a happier hiring manager, this discussion is critical. ➢ Explain (simply and briefly – best not to lecture) what benefits there will be for the search and for your hiring manager. Point out how it will make their life easier. It's easier when they see what's in it for them.

The Consultative Recruiter

BONUS: See the Launch Form I've included for you. It has all the questions that will make your search life much easier—and your hiring managers much happier!	➤ At this point, it probably doesn't work to talk about how it helps you—focus on what is in it for your hiring manager to take the time to have a detailed launch meeting with you. ➤ If your hiring manager doesn't want to make time for this discussion, start with a casual conversation where you can slip in a few of the most critical questions. They will start to see the value of doing a complete launch meeting with you. ➤ Then you can use the **Launch Form** I've included for you to ask all the essential questions about the position—the kinds of questions that can get the hiring manager to begin to see you as a consultant and business partner.
There is no job description for the opening, the description is outdated and/or the hiring manager isn't entirely sure of the qualifications they are looking for.	➤ Use the included **Launch Form**. Those questions will help you guide the hiring manager so the two of you come up with a job description that helps ensure you can be effective and the hiring manager can be happy! ➤ It's interesting to note that it's not always easy for a hiring manager to write a current job description. Even if they do write a job description, you know it won't be the marketing piece you can post. ➤ Use what you hear to develop a job description and a posting. The posting is your marketing piece written to attract your ideal candidates. That is not the purpose of a job description, so it's best to have both. Posting just a job description is sure to slow down your search!
The hiring manager changes their mind about what they are looking for in the middle of a search	➤ The comprehensive **Launch Form** helps the hiring manager set out at the beginning what they are looking for. ➤ When they start to change their mind—adding new requirements and/or responsibilities to the job—you can use what you heard in the launch to get the search back on track or know with confidence what the new direction should be—without damaging the partnership relationship.

16

Hiring manager is out of touch with the competitive realities of the candidate marketplace today, including generational differences, how people view your company, etc.	➢ Share with the hiring manager what you know about the marketplace realities and what it will take to land their ideal candidate. This includes things like increased competition for particular skills, the need to pay more in order to be competitive, etc. ➢ Look for non-confrontational (and non-lecture) ways to let that manager know what they are looking for may not exist, may not fit their company range, etc. Discuss how today's realities may impact the number of candidates who will be interested, the need to relocate a candidate in order to fill the position, to pay more than the current compensation range, etc. ➢ While you may not totally change their perception (or what they say) in just one meeting, keep using the techniques and they will get that your advice is helpful to them. ➢ Rather than say these realities mean the position won't be filled or that it will take a very long time, go for a compromise. See if the hiring manager will agree to let you take the position as defined to the candidate marketplace to see how many qualified candidates raise their hand. Promise to provide the results of your market "research" in the next meeting with them. ➢ Then, you and the hiring manager can meet in a week or so to discuss your market findings and make adjustments as much as possible as required. ➢ One important trusted advisor role is to help the hiring manager understand what is possible in today's economy, whether it's robust or rotten. And then, of course, to figure out how to get the position filled and make the hiring manager your business partner! ➢ Just promise yourself that you will never do a **"I told you so."** While perhaps justified, you will achieve a business relationship much faster if people don't feel that is where you are coming from.

The company, or the compensation committee or the hiring manager don't want to pay a competitive salary and don't believe you when you tell them what it will take.	➤ If you suspect candidates who meet the requirements are not affordable, the launch meeting is a perfect place to start that conversation. As with other potential challenges, it's best to avoid saying there will be no candidates who are in the target comp range. Ya never know! ➤ Mention what you know about the candidate pool and the fact that the best candidates may be outside the compensation range being offered. ➤ Suggest that you bring candidates who are in the range, and a couple who appear to be a great fit but are more expensive. This way, the hiring manager can see what the extra dollars can buy. Then they can decide if they want to see only candidates within the target range, or if they are willing to consider qualified candidates who are above the range. ➤ Nothing will speak as loudly as the data from the market. When you can show great candidates already at or above the compensation your company is offering, the decision makers now have data that supports making a change. ➤ If there isn't going to be a change, it's probably time for a discussion about what requirements can be loosened in order to find a candidate at the compensation range they are willing to pay.
Hiring managers do not feel they get to see enough quality candidates. **NOTE:** In these situations, hiring managers have a nagging feeling that there are more great candidates out there, but they aren't getting to see them.	➤ One of the scariest questions for us as recruiters to ask is: **How many candidates would you like to see? How many candidates would you have to see in order to feel comfortable that you've seen the best of the best?** (and of course, stop talking once you've asked a question to give your hiring manager time to respond.) ➤ It's really difficult to meet and/or manage expectations when you don't know what they are. If their expectations make sense for this search, you can say something like: "That's seem reasonable. We'll know more once we start to see how candidates respond to the position."

This is a bit different than the situation with a hiring manager who just wants to see more, even though you've sent candidates who met their requirements.	➤ If their expectations are totally off the map, like maybe wanting to see 15-20 candidates for one position, start to build a compromise position. "I'll send you the first 4-5 candidates who look like they are a great fit. Then we can talk about whether you feel you need to see more." Then when you have that meeting, use the techniques in the challenge above when the hiring manager wants to see more candidates. ➤ You'll notice this is one of the questions on the **Launch Form**. It's an essential question that helps ensure you and the hiring manager finish the search quickly and happily.
Hiring manager doesn't make and/or doesn't keep to the necessary timeline. One of the biggest (and universal) time wasters for us as recruiters is waiting for hiring managers to give us the feedback so we can move the search forward appropriately. You can change that with this technique!	➤ After expectations about the timeline are set, commitments have been made that may not get met and/or there needs to be a non-confrontational discussion to get the timeline adjusted appropriately. ➤ Use the "**Sticky Commitment**" technique. That is one of the behaviors that trusted advisor recruiters would use with a business partner. ➤ That doesn't mean you have to "take it" when the HM doesn't get back to you. If the hiring manager misses the deadline THEY set and confirmed, call or visit them within no more than an hour of missing the deadline. Don't just sit and wait for them to eventually get back to you. ➤ If you do have to do the second question on the Sticky Commitment formula, try to avoid asking that second question in an email. Give it a personal touch, especially if you're nervous about doing it in person or on the phone. It is OK to leave a voice mail—just be sure to use a neutral tone. ➤ It may take a bit of time for them to get used to keeping their commitments to you. Keep expecting them to do that and gently giving them a second chance when they miss their initial commitment; soon they will keep their commitments to you!

	LANGUAGE TIP: Don't keep contacting the HM to get feedback. That will be perceived as **order-taker behavior**. • Use the **Sticky Commitment technique**, and hold them to it, gently and with a real intention to make the relationship the priority.
Hiring manager keeps canceling or not showing up for interviews with candidates.	➢ While this makes for a very bad candidate experience, adds to your work load and stretches out the time to fill metric, do not lecture the HM about any of these things. ➢ Use a variation of the Sticky Commitment technique. Even if you have access to the HM calendar and can schedule interviews for them, don't do it if the HM is blowing off interviews. ➢ Ask when it works for them to do the interviews, what gets in the way of doing the interviews, is there any way you can make the interviewing scheduling easier for them, etc. There may be a valid reason this is happening, and as their business partner, you can help them resolve this. **LANGUAGE TIP:** Recognize: • That even though you're irritated by this, **go into the conversation** (phone or in person, never email for this one) with the intention to resolve it so it works for the HM and of course the candidates. • This approach goes a long way to encourage the HM to work with you to get these interviews to happen, so everyone wins!
Hiring managers drag their feet at decision time.	➢ It's helpful to explore at the beginning of a search how many candidates the HM needs to see before making a decision. ➢ *Ask this question:* ❑ If the first candidate you interview is a good fit and meets the requirements, would you be willing to make an offer?

- Even if you don't ask, they have some number in mind. No matter how perfect the candidate they hire is, they will often feel uncomfortable that they didn't see whatever number they were thinking would be "enough".

- I've seen situations where a search was filled with one (and the first) candidate. You might think the HM would be delighted they didn't have to spend time interviewing more candidates, got their position filled quickly, etc. The HM was actually angry that he hadn't had more choices.

- If the numbers requirement is met, and still no decisions, you can really help the HM in this situation.

- Now is the time to ask the questions, in a non-push-back manner, that will help the HM think through how each candidate did or did not meet the requirements.

- Plus if you have a HM who is delaying because they fear making a bad hiring decision, you can help them come to a decision they can feel comfortable making.

- One effective tool is to develop a grid with ALL the requirements, plus feedback items you heard from the hiring manager throughout the search. Indicate which qualifications each candidate meets, or do that with the HM. It's important to make sure you and the HM are on the same page about each candidate.

- This exercise will help the HM think through the search. Plus there is real power in having a visual evaluation of the candidates compared to the requirements and compared to each other.

- If the HM is still not willing to make a decision, have a very specific conversation about how the next candidate(s) have to differ from the ones already interviewed. If you don't get that detailed level of specificity, you will be throwing candidates up on the wall to see if they stick for a very long time.

	LANGUAGE TIP: Never respond to these kinds of situations with "OK" and then go away hoping you'll be able to get better results with the next round of candidates.

How to Get a Sticky Commitment!

How to Get Feedback from Your Hiring Managers without having to Chase Them

The secret to getting a commitment: Let your hiring manager make the decision. When you tell them when you need them to get back to you in such and such a time-frame, they may say OK, but that's not a commitment.

The secret to success with this: Don't say anything until they answer your question—no options, no explanations (unless they ask), no filling in the silence while they think, etc. It will be tempting to jump in, but resist.

Getting an Initial Commitment	How to handle a Missed Commitment
Ask the hiring manager when they think they will be able to get back to you with their feedback on (resumes, candidate interviews, decision re hiring, etc.) Don't talk about needing to move quickly, losing candidates, etc. They get it even though they may not act as though they do.	"When we talked you thought it would work for you to get back to me in X (days, hours, etc.). That doesn't seem to work for you. What would be better for you?" Be sure not to sound snarky, frustrated or angry when you ask (even though I would understand if you feel that way!) And ask this question right after they miss the commitment deadline they agreed to.
Now the hard part: **Don't say anything else until they answer you.** Let them make their decision because that's how you get a commitment. Lather, Rinse, Repeat	**Now the hard part:** **Don't say anything else until they answer you.** Let them make a decision because that's how you get a commitment. Lather, Rinse, Repeat

When the HM doesn't seem to have a sense of urgency, you get to take ....A Soft Pause

When you start a search or at least before submitting candidates, determine how quickly the HM wants the position filled. **Ask this question** (even if you know what they are going to say): When would it be ideal to have this filled?
And of course, now the hard part: Don't say anything else until they answer you.

Later, when the HM seems to be losing momentum and slowing things down, you say:

"When we talked, you were thinking you wanted to fill this as quickly as possible. But if that timeframe is not relevant any more, no problem. I'll just go on a soft pause until you have a chance to get me the feedback that lets me know what the next steps should be.

Of course, if someone great shows up, I'll certainly bring them to you, but in the meantime, I'll just go on soft pause."

Now you have to do two hard things: **Don't say anything else until they answer you AND don't do a lecture about urgency. That is not the route to influence.**

Search Launch Document

POSITION PROFILE	
Position Title: Location: # of openings:	Compensation: Base Bonus Other Exempt: Yes __ No__
Hiring Manager:	Hiring Manager's Title:
Hiring Manager Email: Hiring Manager Phone:	Preferred communication method:
HR Business Partner:	HRBP Preferred Communication method:
__ New Position __ Replacement	Name of Previous Employee: Terminated ___ Resigned ___
Travel %: _____	
Travel to where:	For what purposes:
Will considering relocating a candidate __ Yes __ No__ Relocation Assistance Package? __ Yes No__	
Position Level for benefits etc: __ Executive __ Director __ Manager	

INTERNAL/EXTERNAL FACTORS

☐ Internal candidates only ☐ External candidates only ☐ Internal and External candidates

Additional info about why this position is available: Is this a newly defined position? Is it open as a result of business growth/redirection? Did the previous person get promoted?	
Background/qualifications of predecessor What was missing?	
Success factors of predecessor or the best people in the position.	
What do/did they do that was better than expected?	
What traits would the hiring manager like to have replicated in the new person?	

POSITION DETAILS

Position Overview	
Responsibilities and job duties	
Experience and background of the ideal candidate (required, desired, helpful)	
Job objectives to be achieved within first 90 days, 6 months, first year—whatever is the first evaluation point. Which is the most important; what makes it the most important?	

POSITION DETAILS

What is the most important task for this position? What makes it important to you?	
What are the key issues this person would need to address short-term? Longer-term? Internal and external?	
Key challenges to be met in this role	
Any challenges to success? Internal? External?	
How does this position fit into the long-term strategic goals for the organization?	
Competencies (softer skills, e.g., leadership, team player, self-motivated, etc.)	
What makes this a great career opportunity?	
What makes it exciting to the types of candidates you are looking to attract?	
Career growth potential (either promotionally, acquiring new skills, etc.)	

THE TEAM

If there is someone on the team who feels this position should be theirs, are they a viable candidate? If not, what are they missing that makes them not a fit for the role	
Does this position manage a team and/or supervisor others?	
If so, what titles report to the position? How many of each?	
How many people are on this team?	
What titles/jobs are a part of this team?	
What are the dynamics of the team? What is the culture of the team?	
Is the team fully functional and performing at the level you want them to reach?	
Are there issues with the team, e.g., morale, need to replacement, training, performance, etc.?	
Will there be a need to increase the team in the short term?	
How many years of experience of management would you like to see this person have? Ideal size of teams they will have managed?	

THE COMPANY, CULTURE AND MANAGER

What is happening in the company overall, this portion of the company, this department, etc., that would be important and/or interesting for the candidate to know?	
What does the near term future look like? What new things are you planning? What are you excited about in your business?	
How would you describe the culture today? What is it like to work in this group?	
What are you like to work for? What is your personal style, preferred management style, etc.?	
For relatively new managers, what specifically made you join the company? What are you most enjoying about the company and your role?	

SOURCING

Has the hiring manager asked their employees for referrals? Employee referral program?	
Target Companies (competitions, parallel industries, end users)	

Companies not of interest (because of their culture, business practices, etc., that would make employees incompatible with us)	
Are there companies with whom there are strategic partnerships, vendor relationships, etc., that would make it inappropriate for us to hire someone from that company?	
Will the hiring manager post on their own LinkedIn, do they have any referrals networks, etc.	
What associations does the hiring manager belong to that would include potential candidates for this role?	

PRE-SCREENING INFORMATION

Are there 3 – 5 key questions you would like me to ask candidates as a part of our screening process? (Be sure to ask them how to identify a good answer.)	1. 2. 3.
What is one question that you would like me to ask in the phone interview and what would be a great answer to look for?	
Are there key categories of people you are looking for (e.g., hard charger, creative, intellectually curious, etc.)?	
If so, how do you define those terms?	

PRE-SCREENING INFORMATION

How do you know when you're sitting across from a great candidate?	
If I handed you a resume what would be on it that would make that person an ideal candidate for this role?	
If your ideal candidate is the first person you interview, would you be willing to move them to an offer? If not, how many candidates do you think you would need to see in order to feel you've seen the best available candidates in the marketplace?	

Resume Review Process

How does the hiring manager want to receive resumes for review, e.g., one at a time via email, once a week in a phone call or meeting with you, when you have a certain number ready for review, etc.?	
If the hiring manager has been slow getting you the necessary feedback in the past, ask what would make that step easier for them	
How soon, on average, will the hiring manager get back to you on resumes?	

INTERVIEW STRUCTURE & PROCESS

☐ Round 1 Interview	☐ Phone Interviewer(s):	☐ Individual	☐ Panel	Targeted #:
☐ Round 2 Interview	☐ Phone Interviewer (s):	☐ Individual	☐ Panel	Targeted #:
☐ Round 3 Interview	☐ Phone Interviewer(s):	☐ Individual	☐ Panel	Targeted #:

If the first candidate interviewed meets all the requirements and seems to be a great fit, would you be willing to move to offer stage? If not, what would be the reason? If you want to see more candidates, how many would be sufficient for you to know you're making the right decision?	
After each interview, when do you think you will be able to provide feedback and outline next steps, if any, for the candidate?	
What will be the first step in the process? Will you want us to meet the candidate before you meet them?	
If you like the candidate, what are the next steps? Who interviews at each step?	
Will you want to try to have all candidates to interview on the same day? How will that day be structured?	

INTERVIEW STRUCTURE & PROCESS

If holding candidates already in process to find sufficient number of candidates to form a slate is not feasible, are you flexible on moving people through the process rather than hold everyone until a slate is created?	
How long does the typical process take from first interview to offer decision? Is that your ideal timeframe?	
How many candidates do you typically move to 2nd and beyond interviews before choosing a finalist and making an offer?	
Are things like preparing a 90-day business plan, giving a presentation, etc., part of your process?	
Who else needs to be included in the interview process? If they are not available, do you need to wait for them, is there an alternative person or will you just leave them out this time?	
What are the reasons you would like these people to be part of the interview process?	
Have you shared your desired timeline and expectations of the role they will play with everyone?	

INTERVIEW STRUCTURE & PROCESS

Does everyone involved in the interview process understand the position, what is important to be accomplished in the role, experience required, etc? Have they seen and/or had input into the posting?	
Are you asking certain people to interview for certain experiences, qualities, etc., of the candidate? Do the interviewers know your expectations of what they will be looking for?	
Does everyone involved in the interview process have a vote? Who gets a vote and who just gets to have an opinion? Do they know?	
How do you collect feedback from the other interviewers?	
What is the biggest benefit you get as the hiring manager from having this interview process?	

About the Author

Recruiting was a third career for Katherine, after serving as a marketing executive for a software development firm and running her own coaching and personal development firm for several years.

Katherine has been a corporate recruiter, a recruiter for a world-wide retained executive search company as well as a small regional retained recruiting firm. She has done searches for positions ranging from individual contributors to CEOs with million dollar salaries, in industries ranging from complex technologies to cupcakes.

Today Katherine is training and coaching recruiters in companies across the US, including DIRECTV, Verizon Wireless, Avery Dennison and The Cheesecake Factory.

Even though it means leaving her lakeside cabin, she is excited to meet recruiters around the country and see how her techniques are helping them fill positions faster. And even more exciting--they report they are having more fun and enjoying more influential relationships with their hiring managers.

Made in the USA
Lexington, KY
05 February 2019